Ecosystems

Wetlands

by Nadia Higgins

Bullfrog Books

Ideas for Parents and Teachers

Bullfrog Books let children practice reading informational text at the earliest reading levels. Repetition, familiar words, and photo labels support early readers.

Before Reading

- Discuss the cover photo. What does it tell them?

- Look at the picture glossary together. Read and discuss the words.

Read the Book

- "Walk" through the book and look at the photos. Let the child ask questions. Point out the photo labels.

- Read the book to the child, or have him or her read independently.

After Reading

- Prompt the child to think more. Ask: Have you ever visited a wetland? Have you seen videos or pictures? How would you describe it?

Bullfrog Books are published by Jump!
5357 Penn Avenue South
Minneapolis, MN 55419
www.jumplibrary.com

Library of Congress Cataloging-in-Publication Data

Names: Higgins, Nadia, author.
Title: Wetlands / by Nadia Higgins.
Description: Minneapolis, MN: Jump!, Inc., [2017]
Series: Ecosystems
"Bullfrog Books are published by Jump!"
Audience: Ages 5–8. | Audience: K to grade 3.
Includes bibliographical references and index.
Identifiers: LCCN 2016059612 (print)
LCCN 2017000032 (ebook)
ISBN 9781620316832 (hardcover: alk. paper)
ISBN 9781620317365 (pbk.)
ISBN 9781624965609 (ebook)
Subjects: LCSH: Wetland ecology—Juvenile literature. | Wetlands—Juvenile literature.
Classification: LCC QH541.5.M3 H54 2017 (print)
LCC QH541.5.M3 (ebook) | DDC 577.68—dc23
LC record available at https://lccn.loc.gov/2016059612

Editor: Jenny Fretland VanVoorst
Book Designer: Molly Ballanger
Photo Researcher: Molly Ballanger

Photo Credits: Alamy: Malcolm Schuyl, 14–15. Getty: Grant Dixon, 10–11; Gary Meszaros, 16. Shutterstock: J. Marquardt, cover; tea maeklong, 1; Robert Eastman, 3; Romrodphoto, 5; Africa Studio, 12; Serg Zastavkin, 13; FloridaStock, 17; Lynn Whitt, 19; GUDKOV ANDREY, 20–21; jpcuadrado, 23tr; Eric Isselee, 23ml; Madlen, 23mr; lazyllama, 23br; Narupon Nimpaiboon, 24. SuperStock: Don Johnston/age fotostock, 4; Minden Pictures, 6–7; Tom Till, 8–9; Rene Krekels/NiS/Minden Pictures, 15; Wolfgang Kaehler, 18–19.

Printed in the United States of America at Corporate Graphics in North Mankato, Minnesota.

Table of Contents

Wet and Soggy

A wetland is a soggy place.

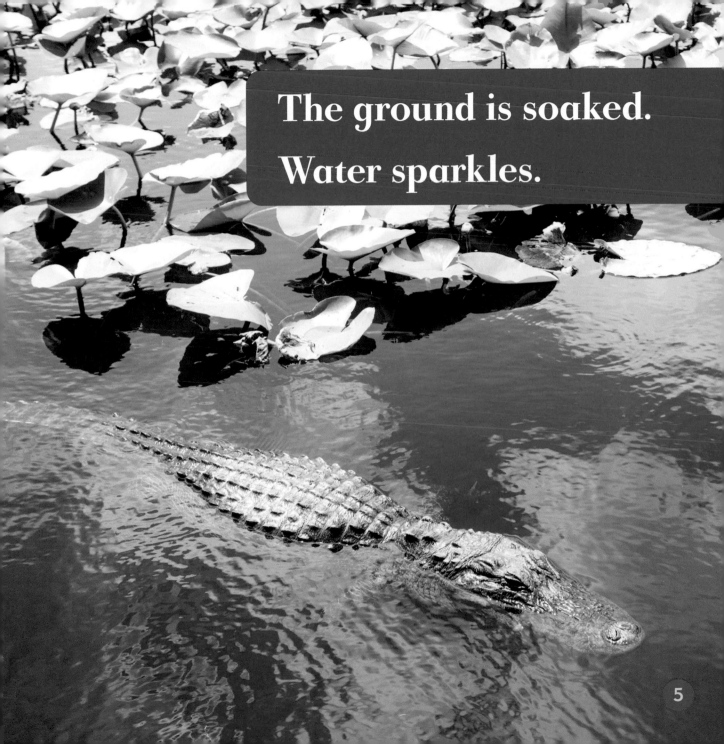

The ground is soaked.

Water sparkles.

But a wetland
is not a lake.

Why not?

The water comes
and goes.

Most plants would
die in soil this wet.

Not wetland plants.

They love it!

Trees grow in a swamp.
Look!
Their roots stick out.
They hold up the tree.

roots

Grasses grow in a marsh.

Mosses grow in a bog.

moss

13

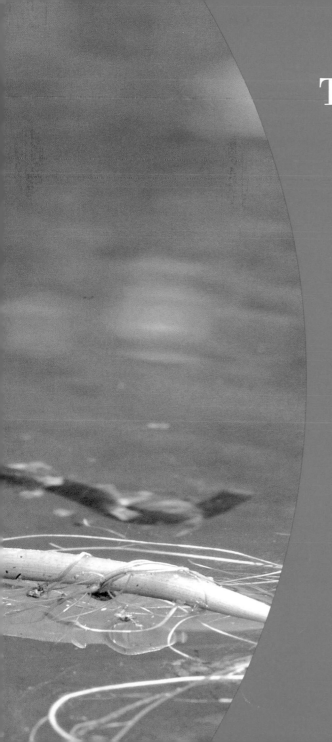

The water is so still.
Insects can
lay their eggs.

eggs

So can frogs.
They eat the insects.

Then bigger animals eat them.

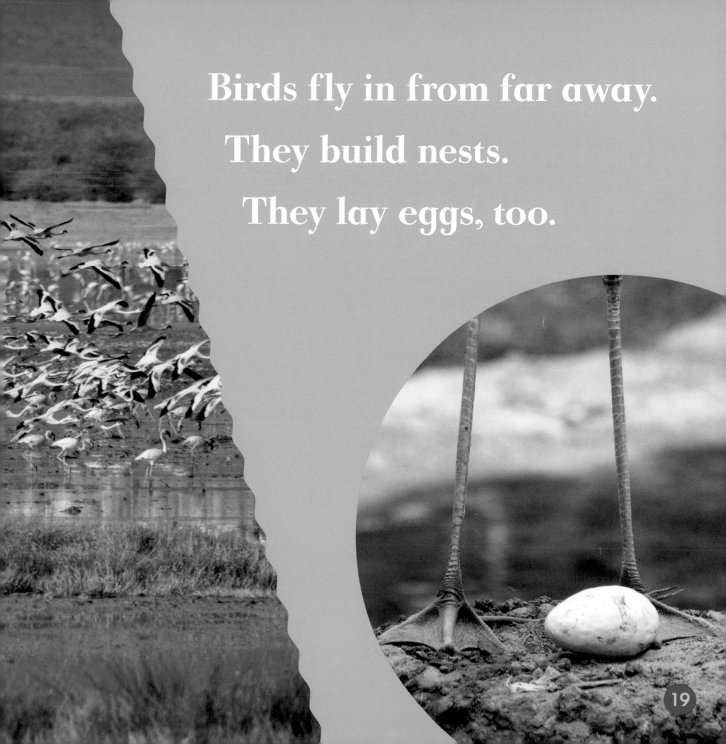

Birds fly in from far away.

They build nests.

They lay eggs, too.

Baby birds will hatch.
They will join this
busy, soggy world.

Where Are the Wetlands?

Wetlands are usually close to bodies of water. Coastal wetlands lie along oceans. Inland wetlands can be found near lakes and rivers.

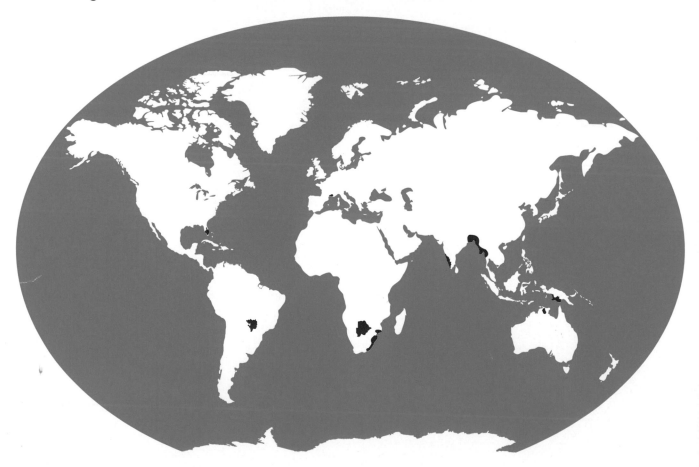

■ areas of important and widespread wetland

Picture Glossary

bog
A kind of wetland where a thick layer of plants grows over the water.

marsh
A kind of wetland where mostly grasses grow.

hatch
To come out of an egg.

soil
Another word for dirt.

insects
Another word for bugs.

swamp
A kind of wetland where mostly trees grow.

Index

To Learn More

Learning more is as easy as 1, 2, 3.

1) Go to www.factsurfer.com

2) Enter "wetlands" into the search box.

3) Click the "Surf" button to see a list of websites.

With factsurfer.com, finding more information is just a click away.